The
HANDBOOK
for
MITIGATION

Purple Feather Press
IMAGINATIVE AND CREATIVE PUBLISHING

The
HANDBOOK
for
MITIGATION

A PRACTICAL GUIDE FOR
THE COMMUNITY
AROUND A CRIMINAL CASE

VICTORIA RUSK

The HANDBOOK *for* MITIGATION

Rusk, Victoria
The Handbook for Mitigation: A Practical Guide for the Community Around a Criminal Case.

Printed in the United States. Updated 2025.

ISBN: 978-1-959600-07-7

Purple Feather Press
Georgetown, Texas
www.PurpleFeatherPress.com

Originally published in the United States by MILA INK, Huntsville, AL.

Original Cover and Text Design: Henry Baring

Original ISBN: 978-0-578-76154-1

TESTIMONIALS

"I think you make it very clear that the circumstances of the crime are not the same as the circumstances of the person."

"I like the points you made about 'healthy brains don't hurt people.' So true! Brain damage and impulsivity are at the root cause of so many criminal cases."

"Your discussion about trauma is terrific. Realizing that trauma isn't always some disastrous physical event. The trauma of being marginalized, of being stigmatized & living in poverty. Nicely Done!"

Mitigation Specialist
Joe Guastaferro

The Handbook for Mitigation is a fantastic explanation of mitigation that would be very useful for clients and their loved ones. The fabulous part of the book is its simplicity making the mystery of mitigation open up for all to understand. The book also has helpful tips for attorneys in working with mitigation.

The part that I got the most out of was the section discussing the documents that you give the attorneys. If I could get a packet like that my life would be so much easier.

Attorney Sandra Hamilton
Phoenix, AZ

Victoria us able to describe how emotional this process can be. She helped me know how to navigate a case with heart. In this book you learn how beneficial it is to have accessible mitigation assistance.

It's the heart of the case.

As a family member of someone who has gone through the court system I would recommend this book to everyone. Anyone can gain insight on how important mitigation is to the end result. Mitigation brings forth the humanity of the person, and that's the most important thing.

Elizabeth Ligas

"The work of a mitigation consultant, someone who knows the connections between trauma and behavior, the science behind these connections, and who understands the ways in which those connections may figure in each criminal defense case, is what blends the data with the principles and produces solid mitigation outcomes. I applaud Ms. Rusk for this excellent little manual. I am holding onto my copy, but I'm passing around a few others to folks who need to know what wise, cooperative and courageous witnesses know."

Attorney Suzie Mindlin

"Injustice anywhere is a threat to justice everywhere."

- MARTIN LUTHER KING JR.

Acknowledgements

My most grateful thanks are due to Treanor Baring editor and accountability partner, Henry Baring for his design and personal touch. For the people who participated in the book's focus group: I appreciate your time, energy and investment: Eric Allen, Linda Gilmore, Dr. John Rodriquez, Jade Aslain, Domnique Clark, Margie Graves, Rob Wells, Donald Gallick, Cynthia Short, Tim Weston, Victoria Cruz, and Zach Pruitt. Big thanks to the case law researchers Avery Rios and Avery Aiken.

TABLE OF CONTENTS

FOREWORD

My name is Tynice Hall and I'm from Lubbock, Texas. I met Victoria over 30 years ago in elementary school. When she got picked on, I was like a bodyguard for her because I've always hated bullies. She was always there for me when my life got complicated. Her house was my go-to escape as a child. We had a strong bond all our school years. We still do.

My upbringing was rough. I fought a lot as a teen, and even was detained in a youth center for a few weeks after I badly injured another girl. I got sent to an alternative school. I never really had anyone to talk to growing up, but I always had Victoria.

Then, when I was 22, on February 23rd, 2006, I was at the right place at the wrong time: my own home. I had a drug-dealing boyfriend who had been under investigation for four years. On that February day, the federal government raided thirty-eight other residences, and five of my boyfriend's stash houses. They found firearms and drugs in my house and arrested me. I was charged with conspiracy to possess and distribute more than 50 grams of crack cocaine, possession of 50 grams or more of crack cocaine base, possession of 50 grams of more with intent to distribute, felony possession of a firearm, and conspiracy.

I couldn't afford a lawyer, so the court appointed one. I was naïve. I thought they'd listen to me. Help me. Advise me on what to do. Believe me when I told them I had nothing to do with my boyfriend's business dealings. My lawyer was from one of the best firms in my area, but I never got to see that. My attorney told me to tell the authorities what they wanted to hear.

But I didn't know anything. My lawyer never asked me about me. I kept thinking justice would prevail and I wanted to take my case to trial. I was found guilty. Just five months after I'd been arrested, on my birthday, July 27th, I was sentenced to thirty-five years in federal penitentiary.

While I was incarcerated, Victoria started studying mitigation, and she explained it to me. I think if I'd had a mitigation specialist on my team, I wouldn't have received thirty-five years in the penitentiary.

I'm not alone. What happened to me happens to other women all the time. A friend of mine started an organization to help women given harsh sentences. Several other criminal justice organizations and some famous people rallied around me. On February 18, 2020, I received clemency from the President of the United States. Finally, my story was heard. I hope this book helps others get their story heard, too.

INTRODUCTION

Life is an ongoing exploration. A mitigation specialist in criminal defense is in the business of understanding the basics of a person's life, their family of origin story, their experiences in school, jobs, relationships, and how he or she lived those experiences. Every life has a story.

This book shares my life's work as a mitigation specialist, and the outcomes I've witnessed from my experience so far. I will share my professional know-how and my interpretation of what mitigation is, and how it can work in criminal defense. My goal in writing this is to make mitigation accessible in as many cases as possible, one day in all of them. This book is for anyone interested in mitigation. It's intended as a tool for people to read, to learn from, to take in the information and utilize my background, my experience, my knowledge and to make it their own.

Criminal defense is a place for warriors, humanitarians, and storytellers. I see myself as all three. I think I was always meant to be in mitigation. The path I took may seem winding at first, but looking back, I believe it was always leading straight toward criminal defense. I've worked in a variety of fields, one being new home construction, where I met formerly incarcerated people. The construction job was the job between jobs, to make ends meet, but I'm so glad I had it! Previously, I worked for the Epilepsy Foundation, where I learned how unique the brain is. Before that, I worked in Guam as a lifeguard. My first job was in journalism for six years. I did say it was a winding path, right?

Every experience contributed to who I have become and to how I practice mitigation. With every step in my professional development, I gained know-how and skills that I apply to my work today. I'm not alone. Most of the attorneys I work with have had life experiences that make them passionate about this work. They have chosen to be the first responders to events that shock, anger, and even traumatize those involved. The attorneys I work with have one thing in common, they believe in fairness. They also know, like me, that justice does not come easy. It must be based on our common humanity. There's heartbreak and meaning in the untold stories.

I grew up in Lubbock, Texas, the middle girl between two brothers. My parents got divorced when I was six years old. I lived mostly with my mom on 65th street, one block from the projects. I had a close relationship with a wide community of family and friends. I was also close to my dad, a trucker. All the people who loved me kept me safe. They are my foundation and how I became a courageous woman. They taught me what it meant to give to others, to look after our neighbors. When they saw someone in trouble, they helped. It came naturally to them, and now that is deeply ingrained in me, not to just walk by someone in need.

I had to work hard growing up to earn money. I babysat, cleaned houses. I did whatever work I could find. I was the first person in my family to go to college. The jobs I had in my twenties (television news producer, spokesperson, construction worker), let my friend to think I would be a natural fit for mitigation. He sent my resume to the public defender's office. I was hired after two interviews. I believe the hiring manager appreciated that my heart, my passion, and my skills from other jobs were leading me to a career in mitigation. I was trained in West Texas and later moved to Houston. I've been working in mitigation for death penalty cases ever since.

I've always been "all in" with the job of mitigation specialist, and "all in" is how I'm writing this book. My goal is to bring this information to life. All my experiences have brought me here. This expertise and understanding can help others.

Which brings me to something I want to share: the spiritual dimension at the heart of mitigation investigation. It involves following your heart, trusting the process, the people, sometimes even having blind trust in the people in the case. Most of all, it means letting go of expectations and allowing the case to unfold. Mitigation investigation is the process of solving the mystery of motivation of an individual person in a unique situation.

Mitigation investigation follows leads from people and records. There's no guarantee that those people and records are going to exist, or that you'll have access to them, and when they do, you do not know what you are going to find. There is a huge amount of faith and trust in the equation of mitigation. Why does one witness talk and another won't? Why is it that every record shows an address is correct, but no one is ever home? Once, I got three addresses for one person, and thankfully, the person at one address knew where to find the other. Why does one institution have records from thirty-five years ago but another institution shreds records after five years? Why does one family member love the grandmother, but the rest of the family hates her? How many interviews does it take for a person to open up? How do you know what information will touch a jury to choose life over death? The different answers are found in each case. These are the mysteries that can only be uncovered with the exercise of trust and faith. Persistence is key. Belief in a big picture is a must. Mitigation is full of miracles. No two human beings are alike. Every case is unique. Integrity is everything.

Chapter 1: This Book is for You

This book is for the community around a case. In this book, you'll learn about the winning formula for sentencing for criminal defense. You'll also learn what you can do for the accused person in the case you're involved in. You will learn about the roles of the defense team members, the investigation process, and mitigating evidence. I also hope you will come away understanding the *why* and *how* you should, and can, contribute to fair punishment in our criminal justice system.

A criminal case is more than a collection of individuals working on the prosecution or the defense sides. There's a team representing the state, or the people, and another team working on behalf of the accused. There are also independent players, such as judges, jurors, and court personnel. Behind every case there are police officers, witnesses, victims and their families, and the accused and their families.

Strangers will find their paths crossing. They will form a community, whether they know it or not. The best relationships between attorneys and a community, including the client, develop when trust is established. Everyone in the case is a human being. Mitigation investigation focuses on the *why* beneath the crime. It humanizes the accused to the independent decision makers, who the public knows as the jury or the judge.

Chances are, if you're reading this book, you're a part of a team that can help bring about a fair and peaceful outcome. You may have been given this book by an attorney, you may be an attorney, or you may be someone looking to become a mitigation specialist. You might be reading this book because you are accused of a crime. Perhaps your attorney talked with you about mitigation and handed you this book and you're wondering how it can help. You might not know it, but you can have a mitigation specialist as well as an investigator. However you come to read this, my goal is to give you a sense of mitigation at its best and some concrete ways you can make a difference yourself.

If you are related to someone accused of a crime, read this book to learn what mitigation can do to help your loved one and what you can do to participate in mitigation. At the early stages of a case, you will have more questions than answers. You may feel powerless, but you are not. If you can, hire an attorney immediately after your loved one is charged. If you can't afford an attorney, then an attorney will be appointed after arraignment (formal reading of the charges in a court). Even if you aren't as close to the accused as a husband or wife, mother or brother, this book can help because we all play a role.

What happens when you see someone you care about on the evening news under arrest for a heinous crime? You're in shock, scared for them, ashamed of knowing this person because the news story is so dreadful. Then, someone called a mitigation specialist gets in touch with you. "Can you talk about your former student, your friend, your employee?" they ask. If you find yourself as a mitigation witness, reading this book will help you understand more about what to expect and how to help the accused person.

If you are a defense attorney reading this book, I want you to win justice for your client. Mitigation is a powerful tool that can lead you toward success in very challenging cases and situations. It is also your role as the head of the defense team to introduce mitigation to the client, witnesses, prosecutor, and judge. I write this book for you and the people you come in contact with every day. If you've spent any time at all trying to explain to members of your team, or the client's community, what mitigation is and how it will be used, you know how important it is for everyone to understand.

All attorneys could have at least ten copies of this book to give away. This book is a shortcut that can prevent attorneys from having to repeat the same information over and over. Attorneys, your time is valuable, and if this book saves you hours, I have done my job. Whether you are a seasoned capital defense attorney with years of experience with mitigation or this is the first case where you believe mitigation could be helpful, this book can help you explain the power of mitigation.

Mitigation specialists, I want our work to be understood. Mitigation is complex. My goal is to provide as much information as possible in an accessible and understandable way. When clients and witnesses know what we know about our field, our work will be seamless. Mitigation specialists can hand this book out to their clients. Give it to anyone you think should have it. You can discern who can benefit, who needs it most, and how to use it.

We have all been shaped by relationships and circumstances that brought us to where we are today. Mitigation evidence exists at the heart of every single case and every single life. Everyone has a story to tell. No matter who you are or why you are reading this book, I hope you will come away knowing what mitigation is and how it can be used in the criminal justice system. Most of all, how *you*, no matter how powerless, ashamed, or angry you might feel, can make a difference.

Chapter 2: Mitigation Defined

The basic dictionary definition of mitigation is "making something less severe, dangerous, painful, harsh, or damaging."[1] In the context of a criminal case, that "something" is the sentence or punishment. So, mitigation in criminal defense is the process of making sentences and punishments fair for the accused person. For me, mitigation is really biography. We aren't mitigating the crime—we can't make that less painful, harsh or damaging. In the business, we say, "we mitigate the person, not the crime." We humanize the accused. We tell the story of their human experience. We aim to present the decision makers with the information and viewpoint they need to make a moral decision on punishment.

Although criminal investigation has been around in some form for centuries, the modern concept of professional and independent crime investigations and forensics only became common in the 20th century.[2] Prosecutors, police officers, and investigators on the prosecution side are focused on finding out the *who, what, where, when,* and *how*. They look for the aggravating circumstances of crime, factors that are used by the prosecution to argue for a harsher sentence. But, what about on the other side of the coin? The *why* behind the crime? Mitigation.

There may be a defense investigation into the *who, what, where,* and *how*, but mitigation investigations, along with how these facts are experienced, expand far beyond the

---

1 "Mitigation." Merriam-Webster.com Dictionary, Merriam-Webster, https://www.merriam-webster.com/dictionary/mitigation. Accessed 29 May. 2020.

2 Braga, A., Flynn, E, et al. "Moving the Work of Criminal Investigators Towards Crime Control," *New Perspectives in Policing*, Harvard Kennedy School Program in Criminal Justice Policy and Management and the National Institute of Justice, March 2011. Retrieved from https://www.ncjrs.gov/pdffiles1/nij/232994.pdf

crime. Mitigation investigations gather and present evidence of "mitigating factors" from the client's whole life to secure a fair trial and sentencing for the client. Mitigation asks a judge or jury to look beyond the immediate loss and consider the significant life circumstances leading up to a crime.

Mitigation does not seek to excuse the actions of an individual. It aims to help decision makers determine a fair punishment based on a whole person. Understanding mitigation is just as important for a potential juror or decision maker as it is for a defense attorney and defendant. All attorneys must prepare for punishment, even if they know their client is innocent, because the judge or jury are the decision makers. They will have the final word, and mitigation investigation should be a part of the plan from the beginning of a case.

I became a professional mitigation specialist in Texas, a state with one of the highest rates of death sentences and executions in the country. No matter how you feel about the death penalty, or mass incarceration, we all have an interest in a fair criminal justice system. The rights of an accused person are protected under the law and the constitution. This is where mitigation really makes a difference. It balances the scales of justice. It does this through defense teams. It gives attorneys the opportunity to advocate effectively for their clients. To do this, legal defense teams need resources and an understanding of how mitigation works.

Mitigation is the process that gives truth, the whole truth, its voice. I didn't always know I'd be working in criminal defense as a mitigation specialist, but now that I've found this purpose, I believe I have an obligation to share what I know for the benefit of others. The knowledge I've gained shouldn't be limited to the specialists already in the field. What about the people who aren't professionals, the people who haven't chosen to be a part of a case but find themselves faced with the great machine that is the criminal justice system?

During a criminal case, I've come in contact with a lot of vulnerable people. They are hurt and scared and hungry for information. I'm writing this book to communicate what I've learned with those who need it most. Understanding mitigation will make a difference to clients, to family members, to potential witnesses, or to anyone involved in a criminal case.

Historically, mitigation has focused on the most critical of mitigation needs—death penalty cases. Keep in mind that mitigation can also help bring about just sentences for many other criminal charges. From the time the death penalty was restored, until the early 2000s, attorneys didn't really have any guidelines about how to investigate, present, or use mitigation evidence. A lack of mitigation resulted in ineffective assistance of counsel and unjust outcomes.[3]

In a series of decisions in the 1970s, the Supreme Court ruled that decision makers, whether juries or judges, should consider mitigating factors:

> The Supreme Court has ruled that in deciding between the death penalty and life in prison, the jury may consider any mitigating evidence a juror finds relevant. The jury is instructed to weigh the mitigating factors presented by the defense against the aggravating factors presented by the prosecution.[4]

This legally required defense teams to put the necessary information in front of the judge or jury for a just sentence for each person.

---

3 Stetler, R. and Wendel, W. (2013). "The ABA Guidelines and the Norms of Capital Defense Representation" *Cornell Law Faculty Publications.* 631.
https://scholarship.law.cornell.edu/facpub/631
4 Mitigation in Capital Cases, retrieved from https://capitalpunishmentincontext.org/issues/mitigation

The American Bar Association (ABA), published guidelines for capital murder cases in 2003 and has updated them since. The guidelines say the defense team *must* conduct a full investigation into the client's entire life. In June 2020, the United Supreme Court found that an attorney for a death penalty case who did not investigate the client's life, including his childhood, had provided ineffective assistance of counsel.[5]

They give examples of records that would need to be searched: medical, educational, correctional, military, and more. The guidelines point to health conditions and mental illnesses, disabilities, and even racial and socio-economic factors as relevant influences. It also describes the qualities needed in a professional mitigation specialist.[6]

The ABA guidelines set forth mitigation guidelines, and attorneys discovered the client's story to make sure lawyers were doing their jobs and the system could provide fair trials. In 2008, the ABA guidelines specifically outlined the required elements of mitigation:

> The defense team must conduct an ongoing, exhaustive, and independent investigation of every aspect of the client's character, history, record and any circumstances of the offense, or other factors, which may provide a basis for a sentence less than death. The investigation into a client's life history must survey a broad set of sources and includes, but is not limited to: medical history; complete prenatal, pediatric and adult health

5 Weiss, D. (2020). "Defense lawyer who didn't probe death-row client's bad childhood was deficient, SCOTUS says." https://www.abajournal.com/news/article/capital-lawyer-who-didnt-probe-clients-bad-childhood-was-deficient-supreme-court-says

6 ABA Guidelines for the Appointment and Performance of Defense Counsel in Death Penalty Cases, GUIDELINE 10.11 – THE DEFENSE CASE: REQUISITE MITIGATION FUNCTIONS OF THE DEFENSE TEAM, 2008, https://www.americanbar.org/groups/committees/death_penalty_representation/resources/aba_guidelines/2008-supplementary-guidelines/2008-guideline-10-11/
For a more extensive review of the history of these mitigation guidelines, and the legal cases showing mitigation's effects on outcomes, see Appendix A.

information; exposure to harmful substances in utero and in the environment; substance abuse history; mental health history; history of maltreatment and neglect; trauma history; educational history; employment and training history; military experience; multi-generational family history, genetic disorders and vulnerabilities, as well as multi-generational patterns of behavior; prior adult and juvenile correctional experience; religious, gender, sexual orientation, ethnic, racial, cultural and community influences; socio-economic, historical, and political factors.[7]

Adopting ABA guidelines for capital cases was a major step to ensure that courts would provide a fair and all-inclusive trial for the best attempt to prevent a death sentence. Since then, practice of attorneys and mitigation specialists have created additional procedures and ethics to further the success of mitigation on a variety of cases.

The U.S. Constitution guarantees right to trial and effective counsel, protecting the client's rights during all phases of the case. This includes the plea stage (Lafler v. Cooper, Fyre v. Missouri), the mitigation investigation, in both capital (Wiggins v. Smith, Rompilla v. Beard) and non-capital cases (Shanklin v. State), plus the presentation of evidence (McCoy v. Louisiana), and the overall right to an effective attorney (Strickland v. Washington). Some of these responsibilities need to be hired out to other professionals. *See more about these cases in the Appendix.*

For the best possible outcome, it's vital to seek out a mitigation specialist almost as soon as attorneys are

---

7 ABA Guidelines for the Appointment and Performance of Defense Counsel in Death Penalty Cases, GUIDELINE 10.11 – THE DEFENSE CASE: REQUISITE MITIGATION FUNCTIONS OF THE DEFENSE TEAM, 2008, https://www.americanbar.org/groups/committees/death_penalty_representation/resources/aba_guidelines/2008-supplementary-guidelines/2008-guideline-10-11/

appointed on a case. Mitigation investigation fulfills certain responsibilities regarding sentencing and preserving a client's rights. Most attorneys do not have the time or law school training to properly investigate and catalog mitigation for presentation at the penalty phase of a trial. Less established lawyers may seek the assistance of well-established professional groups in their state. It is important for the lawyer to seek funding and employ a competent mitigation specialist to assist with the investigation and cataloging of this important evidence.

The ABA guidelines explain the skills a specialist must possess, including relationship building, interviewing skills, and integrity. Specifically, the ABA guidelines state that:

> [M]itigation specialists must be able to identify, locate and interview relevant persons in a culturally competent manner that produces confidential, relevant, and reliable information. They must be skilled interviewers who can recognize and elicit information about mental health signs and symptoms, both prodromal and acute, that may manifest over the client's lifetime. They must be able to establish rapport with witnesses, the client, the client's family and significant others that will be sufficient to overcome barriers those individuals may have against the disclosure of sensitive information and to assist the client with the emotional impact of such disclosures. They must have the ability to advise counsel on appropriate mental health and other expert assistance.[8]

---

8 ABA Guidelines for the Appointment and Performance of Defense Counsel in Death Penalty Cases, GUIDELINE 5.1 – QUALIFICATIONS OF THE DEFENSE TEAM 2008, https://www.americanbar.org/groups/committees/death_penalty_representation/resources/aba_guidelines/2008-supplementary-guidelines/2008-guideline-5-1/

In a perfect world, the legal field would be flooded with mitigation specialists, who could perform all the duties listed in the ABA guidelines. In the real world, however, there are not yet enough mitigation specialists to fulfill the needs of every accused person charged with a crime. It's not that there aren't enough qualified people in the country; it's that not enough people even know about the field of mitigation.

Since death penalty cases demand the most time and attention, caseloads can become unmanageably high, depending on the situation. In some cities, it depends on who is available and if that case requires out of town travel, not to mention how the case will be funded. Mitigation specialists who possess the skill sets outlined in the ABA guidelines, establishing relationships and understanding mental illness for instance, are an invaluable part of preparation for punishment, no matter how the funding is achieved (private or court appointment).

It is my observation that many judges and attorneys are beginning to recognize the importance of mitigation specialists in fair sentencing. Still, it may not always be possible to appoint a mitigation specialist in various felony cases. In my opinion, before a case goes to trial, and during plea negotiations, are the critical times for presenting mitigation evidence. However, the mitigation investigation occurs months before, so it's important for the mitigation specialist to be brought on board as early as possible. The sooner the better because mitigation brings about more fair or peaceful outcomes. Mitigation discovers themes and important facts that influence and inform an effective defense strategy. I hope the law is catching up to this reality.

CHAPTER 3: THE DEFENSE TEAM

Mitigation and storytelling connect the dots for the decision makers. Defense attorneys work with a team of professionals, such as an investigator, paralegal, mitigation specialist, forensic experts, and other lawyers. These professionals make up what we usually think of as "the defense team." The defense team can also consist of members of the community around the case, the family, witnesses, and the clients themselves. The professionals are all hired to do the job of representing the client. They could be in this line of work because for a variety of reasons. In my experience, defense attorneys believe in justice for all and fighting for the underdog. They want our system to be fair and they believe in serving people who might not otherwise have representation. It's not possible to guess what their motives might be, but keep in mind that these professionals have chosen to work in criminal defense.

As I write this book, most felony defense teams consist of an attorney and an investigator and expert witnesses. For capital murder cases, the team must be appointed two attorneys, one of which is capital qualified, a fact investigator, and a mitigation specialist. Depending on the state and county, one of the attorneys must be capital qualified according to that jurisdiction's guidelines. Each one is a specialist: the attorney in the law, the investigator in fact-finding and double checking the police investigation, and the mitigation specialist in piecing together the puzzle that will form a complete picture of the accused's life.

The Attorney

The lead counsel is the head of the team. The job of defense attorneys is to know the law, argue the law, and protect their clients under the law. To practice law in each state, an attorney must have a law license, and most states require the attorney to be member of that state's bar. The attorney is the only member of the team who can advocate inside the courtroom for their clients' best interest.

The lead attorney will make the major decisions of the case: trial themes, what information is important to present to the judge or jury, as well as how to bargain for a negotiated plea. The attorney also determines what mitigation information is used in the court proceedings. The defense attorney hires professionals to fill in areas of expertise such as mental illness or intellectual disability, confessions, blood splatter, brain injury, childhood trauma, the impact of military combat service, and many other mitigating factors. Each of these professionals contributes to the case, but ultimately, the attorney of record is solely and officially responsible.

The Investigator

The fact investigator investigates the crime and reviews the investigation of the prosecutors/police/detectives. The investigator will conduct an independent investigation in which they interview people and request records to find out what the cops and detectives didn't do. This is the "who, what, where, how, when" of the investigation. They are investigating the facts of the case, the events surrounding the crime. They follow up on leads at the clients' request. They find new witnesses not in the police report. They request phone data and other records to help defend the alleged crime. Defense investigators might re-interview crime witnesses to get more of the story or double-check what the police report states. They are, in effect, investigating the crime for the defense team. They investigate background information and state witnesses, and they may deliver subpoenas.

The Mitigation Specialist

The mitigation specialist and the fact investigator use different approaches to getting information. Fact investigation is a more formal inquiry to examine the facts of the case. Fact investigation outlines the incident or allegation in a linear fashion. Mitigation investigation goes beyond the crime and much deeper into the life history of the accused. This is the "why" investigation. In many cases, the mitigation specialist is able to identify mental health issues for the team. The ABA guidelines require that mitigation specialists "recognize and elicit information about mental health signs and symptoms." [9]

A mitigation specialist rarely visits the crime scene but should be willing to because there could be information there. The mitigation specialist needs to understand the circumstances of the crime and look for mitigation in the crime story. The point is to find mitigating evidence about the accused, not the crime. The crime is one of many tragic events in the person's life. When it comes to discovering their life story, the fact investigative approach is too direct and can actually harm the mitigation process.

Another role of the mitigation specialist is to identify experts for the team and give materials to the expert. The mitigation specialist will gather files of records, documents, expert evaluations, and other materials as part of the mitigation investigation. The mitigation specialist will compile all of this information and deliver it to the attorney. Attorneys request information in a variety of formats.

---

9 ABA Guidelines for the Appointment and Performance of Defense Counsel in Death Penalty Cases, GUIDELINE GUIDELINE 5.1 – QUALIFICATIONS OF THE DEFENSE TEAM 2008, https://www.americanbar.org/groups/committees/death_penalty_representation/resources/aba_guidelines/2008-supplementary-guidelines/2008-guideline-5-1/

If funding is secured, the mitigation specialist's work will continue all the way through the production of the "deliverables," the package of documents, photos, exhibits, timelines, chronologies, and/or a summary report, provided for the attorney. Complex cases, capital murder for instance, need at least 850 hours of mitigation. If funding isn't available or approved, the mitigation specialist will do their best to provide the attorney with what they need to go forward, for example, a detailed to-do list. In court appointed cases, funding is granted or denied by a judge. In private cases, the defendant pays for mitigation services.

Mitigation requires rapport and disclosure, making information -- a lifetime of information -- known. Mitigating factors can be anything. Literally anything that would lead any decision maker to compassion and understanding. When the environment/relationship is good, witnesses will feel comfortable sharing this information, either during investigation or on the stand. A good mitigation specialist will lead with compassion and build rapport long before trial or the preparation of an affidavit. Of all the professionals on the team, the mitigation specialist may have the most contact with the members of the community around the case, the people involved who aren't necessarily trained to work in criminal defense but still can be a part of the team.

Family

These mitigation witnesses are the people involved in the case in a much highly impacted, life-altering way. The client's family, friends, kids, church family, and other mitigation witnesses who may know the client play a major role in the defense. They may not fully understand how the criminal justice system works. They may have never set foot in a courthouse, and they probably have never heard of the word "mitigation." However, what they can share may turn out to be the one thing that saves their loved one from a disproportionate punishment, even death.

Defending the person: Alberto

(all names are fictitious & details of the story altered for privacy)

Alberto was arrested and charged with capital murder for a drive-by shooting. He was the driver and didn't pull the trigger himself. All the same, the prosecutor was seeking the death penalty. I came on the case early on and realized there were a lot of reasons to be hopeful. Alberto was willing to cooperate; that would help. He came from a large family, and they were all on board to do what they could. They had never been treated unfairly by the system, so they had a lot of trust. They also wanted their friends and neighbors to help. Alberto had a big community around him. One obstacle was the professionals simply couldn't communicate with everybody all the time. Some of the family spoke only Spanish, and they didn't all live in the same house or town. We needed one person to act as a go-between for the defense team. Alberto's sister, Aurora, stepped up without us asking. She could see ways to overcome obstacles. Aurora stayed highly involved in the case, in spite of her own emotions. She managed to get past her fear, shame, and disappointment to become an incredible advocate for a fair sentence for Alberto. She translated between Spanish and English, provided a place for people to meet, and helped relatives with a letter writing campaign to the district attorney. I could contact her and be confident that she would share the information with her family. Aurora was able to bring more people into the case, people who wanted to see justice for all. She stayed professional even when it was tough. She was brilliant. Alberto's capital murder charge was downgraded to a different charge. The judge gave him a sentence according to the guidelines for that charge, not for capital murder. Mitigation, along with his and his family's cooperation, saved his life. I'm still friends with Aurora and her family.

Family members are a powerful asset. There will be a lot of relationship building. There will be frustrations, that's ok, mitigation specialists don't take anything you say personally. Once you know what to expect, and what not to expect, you will be able to help your loved one even more.

Wisdom requires an understanding of what we can and cannot control. What we can control is how much we share of ourselves for the betterment of the case. One thing we can't control is the time it takes to put the pieces of the puzzle together. Remember that the defense strategy, the completed puzzle, won't come together overnight. How upfront and vulnerable a witness is willing to be is up to the witness.

The residual emotions that may bubble up during the case may surprise you. As a family member, you are so close to the accused person that the case causes emotional stress and you feel drained. Set boundaries. You aren't letting anyone down. You are helping! You have to take care of yourself to be able to help others. Everyone has a role to play. The first step is to know your role. This takes trust. Trust is built on communication and vulnerability.

Mom, dad, brother, sister, your role is to be cooperative, wise, and brave. Cooperative because we can't represent your loved one (to the best of our ability) without your help. Brave because you're being asked to share information in detail. It takes courage to speak about shame, family drama, love, incest poverty, neglect, and the complexities of your life. Speaking out on topics that affected the development of the loved one or themselves is difficult. You will be tested on a physical and spiritual level through the course of this criminal case. I want to prepare you for it.

As a family member, you should share everything you can with the defense team, even when they can't share information with you. All information is protected. It is confidential. Just like the attorney can't tell you what other people say, they will not share what you say with anyone else. The attorney is a keeper of all the information. The mitigation specialist gathers information for many weeks and months before it can be digested and organized for plea or trial. When the defense team contacts you, you choose if you want to participate in the process. You might still be processing your own emotional response to the alleged crime. You might not think you have anything to offer. Please let the mitigation specialist or attorney determine that by telling them everything.

Over the months, or even years, of a case, the attorney may meet with the family a few times, and the family will also be meeting with other working professionals on the defense team. They will be giving you information and asking for information from you. Some questions you can ask the attorney are:

- How do I get in touch with the team? How will the team get in touch with me?

This seems like a basic question, but you'd be surprised at how many different expectations there are for communication. Some people don't have a phone. Some people don't get voice mail. Some people don't get texts. Some people only use email. Some people don't use electronic communication of any sort.

- What can we know about guilt or innocence?
- What is the range of punishment for the charges?

Even though you haven't been convicted, the attorney must prepare for all 'what ifs.' That means the attorney must prepare for punishment. Allow yourself to have hope while you're open to all conversations and possibilities. The attorney may talk to you about mitigation. You can also bring it up.

- How does mitigation work in a plea bargain?
- What do they think about the judge? How does that judge view mitigation?

These are examples. You'll have other questions. You will not get all the answers you want at the beginning of the process. I apologize for this now. Don't be afraid to ask questions but also don't expect answers to everything you ask. The worst that can happen is the attorney can say, "I don't know," or "I can't tell you that." The attorney can't tell you whether or not the client is provably guilty. The attorney can't predict the future. The attorney can't share the facts of the case or any attorney-client privileged information. This will feel one-sided because it is. Please understand that this is to protect the client and the case. It seems unfair, and it is. The process needs to unfold this way. It takes patience and understanding from you.

In cases where there isn't a mitigation specialist, a family member or advocate of the client can do some things, with permission of the attorney. They can sign a release, or get one signed, so the attorney can obtain records. They might retrieve a variety of records. They can inform people about the case and cut down on the number of back and forth phone calls or confusion when several people have the same questions for the attorney. They can write an affidavit (a sworn statement) or come to court and testify. They can visit the client and provide emotional support (remember all jail mail and phone calls are recorded). This is where the circles of people around a case begin to overlap. There is always a way to help; nothing is too small. The defense team will need all the help they can get, especially when they are working with limited resources. Remember the defense team is often small compared to the prosecution team.

The Client

We are all here for the client. Open letter to Client: I want to be clear with you what you will be deciding for yourself moving forward. A client is only given the power in criminal cases to make the following decisions:

- Will I go to trial or accept a plea?
- If I go to trial, will I testify?
- Will I accept the representation of this lawyer or will I represent myself?
- Is the insanity defense for me?

You will want to hear to the advice of your attorney on all of these even though the decisions are yours. Once you have a lawyer to represent you, all the other decisions belong to the attorney. Including, what defense and strategies will be used in the courtroom.

I know from my experience that before a person is charged with a crime, many terrible things have happened. You've gone through an arrest, an interrogation, a loss of freedom, a realization that your life has drastically changed. The stress that you're under and your reaction to the stress are unique to you. If you're in a situation where you're meeting a mitigation specialist like me, one good thing is that your attorney is preparing a mitigation investigation.

As a common saying goes, "only the truth shall set you free, but first it will hurt." Your role is to share your insights into your life to the best of your ability and connect your team with those who can tell other parts of your story. Sometimes you will succeed at this and at other moments you will fall short. You're on a team, so where you fall short, your team members will pick up the slack. They don't expect you to have all the answers.

Some people have more self-awareness than others and can better share where they are in their life. The more you, the client, trust members of your team, such as your mitigation specialist, the more you'll tell them. The more you share, the better they know you. The more they know you the better they can advocate for you. The more they advocate for you the more the decision makers connect with your story. The more you understand their role, the more you'll be able to help them. Vulnerability takes courage. If you can be gentle with yourself, then you will be gentle with your defense team.

It's possible your punishment will include prison. You may have taken responsibility for what you are accused of if you are guilty. You still deserve to have mitigating evidence presented to the decision makers—judges or jurors. If you are not guilty, you will still need to help with the mitigation investigation because of the possibility that you will be found guilty. This is not easy to read. This is not an easy job. You are not alone. Your story will be told.

Over the course of multiple interviews, your team will build a timeline of your life history, including the names of people who influenced you, for bad or good. If you don't remember everything, don't worry, other people will fill in the gaps. If you cannot make bond and remain in jail, your behavior is important. Hopefully, you will do your best to avoid write-ups. If you're in jail, the mitigation specialist, and other team members, will visit you regularly. If you're out on bond, keeping appointments and being available during the investigation stage is very important.

Other Mitigation Witnesses

The mitigation witness has a variety of important roles to benefit the case and client. Mitigation witnesses sometimes remember things the client doesn't remember or remembers details of a situation outside the control of the client. They are "witnesses" to the accused's life in some way or another. We need witnesses to fill in the pieces of the puzzle. We don't know the client like they do. They are the real experts on the client's life.

They could be family, friends, or the second grade teacher, or the mom's next-door neighbor for ten years, or the co-worker at the client's last job, or the cellmate of the client for a period of time, or the sister, or the ex-husband, or the child of the client. We need to hear their stories, too. These stories are important because they influence the life of the client. We cannot tell the client's whole story without these witnesses.

The contribution of a mitigation witness may be a couple of interviews, an affidavit, a letter, or sometimes sworn testimony. As a mitigation witness, you are a part of a community of people who know the accused, not just for their crime but for who they are as a person. At first, it may be hard for some witnesses to reconcile the crime with what they know about the person accused. They may want to believe there has been a mistake and their friend is really innocent, or they may be confused because they knew both the accused and the victim. They may want to know if the accused is guilty before they will even talk to the defense team. If this is you, it's not your job right now to decide guilt or innocence. You aren't trying to help anyone get away with anything. What you are supposed to do is help bring about a fair result by sharing what you know so the client will be understood.

If you ever cared about the accused person, or they cared for you, this is when they need you the most. You may not even be aware that you know something important.

There can be an internal struggle in sharing negative stories or characteristics about people you know, but the defense team must know everything. There is no good or bad information— it is all just information. The fact that you provide information does not necessarily mean that you will testify. People have an opportunity to influence a case or a person's life, but not everyone will take this opportunity. It depends on the personal journey of each person. It is my hope that, in reading this book, we can leave "all or nothing" merciless punishment out of the equation and work together for fairness.

Defending the person: Jordan
(all names are fictitious & details of the story altered for privacy)

Jordan's case might have seemed cut and dried to an outsider. He had killed several people in a moment of fear, and the prosecutor was going for a death sentence. It was one of those rare, for me at least, cases that went to trial. By that time, I understood the story of his life. I hoped and prayed the jury would feel his life story as I did. Jordan's stepfather, James, said he was willing to help from the beginning. Sometimes people don't know what that really means. It may be easy to say and hard to do, and it was in Jordan's case. Over the course of the case, I built a lot of trust with both Jordan and James. Jordan would say things like, "He has to get rough with me sometimes, so I'd understand." The people around Jordan didn't see that James was abusive. It took a lot of time to get everyone to speak out about what was going on. I told James about my alcoholic stepfather, and James finally opened up about his own childhood. His father had regularly beaten up his mom. James did the same thing to Jordan's mother and eventually Jordan. That kind of trauma is a mitigating factor because it can damage someone's ability to process threats.

Jordan was found guilty by a jury, and that same jury had to decide whether the punishment would be life in prison or death. Twelve mitigating witnesses were prepared to testify, but I knew for Jordan to have a chance with the jury, James would have to take the stand. Up until then, James minimized his abusive behavior. That's natural. But the truth needed to come out from James himself. I told James he could be a hero. I hoped he would come through once he was on the stand. And he did. James testified that he beat Jordan's mother because if she stayed, that meant she loved him. James would even beat their children in drunken rages, including Jordan. He expressed guilt and regret on the stand. The jury understood the trauma Jordan experienced. James was a hero that day.

Every case is different, but every one of them has the need for trust and integrity. All cases begin with a need for rapport between the people involved. Positive relationships built between the professionals and non-professionals can overcome communication barriers and lead to trust. Without trust established, there will be miscommunication. If people don't feel they are heard, or that they can ask questions, trust will suffer. Without integrity, you can't have trust. Without integrity, nothing works. This is true across all cases because it's an overarching ideal. How these factors play out is going to be very different in each case.

Chapter 4: Every Case is Unique

What makes each case different? People, of course. And the jurisdiction. No two people are alike. That's what makes us human. It is the same for jurisdictions. No two cases will ever have the same facts, police reports, witnesses, circumstances, judge, prosecutor, or jurors. The connection of these people to each case will never be the same again. The breakdown and the uniqueness of individual cases goes deep because building trust with someone is special for each person. Just think how each romantic relationship you've experienced is so different from the next. The same pick-up line doesn't work on everyone, right? Even the relationship between a parent and each of their children can vary. If you lump all the cases with the same indictment or charge in a box thinking they're the same, you have missed the point.

It's no secret that the criminal justice system is divided into the haves and have-nots. The most obvious inequality is who can afford an attorney. If an attorney is hired and paid for by the accused or the family, that is a private case. If funding must come from the court, an attorney is appointed. Court appointed attorneys get a bad rep because their caseload is extraordinarily overwhelming. Public defenders' offices are underfunded, and there are never enough resources or time. Court appointed attorneys are another casualty of the system, but the ultimate casualties are the accused who live in the crisis of poverty.

Defending the person: Kelly

(all names are fictitious & details of the story altered for privacy)

I was appointed to Kelly's case in 2015, two years after the alleged crime, a capital offense. When I first met Kelly, I think it was the first time she had even seen her court-appointed attorneys in six months. It is not that the attorneys weren't working on her behalf, but from their point of view, Kelly was difficult. They were doing their best with their caseload and the challenges her case presented, but Kelly was unhappy with how her case was going. I could see how Kelly felt, and I could see how the attorneys had the capacity to help Kelly. They had tried to get Kelly to accept a plea deal, but she didn't accept it, so they gave up trying. She felt abandoned. It was a classic case of lack of trust. The case was going to trial, and I knew there was more to this situation than met the eye, but first, the team had to restore trust between all the members of the community around this case: the family, friends, attorneys, and Kelly, and I knew it would not happen overnight.

So, I started by simply listening. Empathetic listening was the only way to hold open a space for trust while I worked on the investigation. All I could do was to keep building bridges between Kelly and the attorneys and her family. My ultimate job was to find out the truth behind why Kelly was the way she was, and to do that, I had to restore integrity in all the team's interactions. I helped Kelly get the answers she and the family needed. I brought her mom to the jail and waited for 40 minutes while she visited her daughter and then drove her back home. I spent months working in close contact with Kelly's family. I developed a rapport. Slowly, Kelly shared her story. This led me to find people who could testify about her life.

I realized Kelly was one of the most traumatized people I'd ever worked with. She couldn't trust anyone. The attorneys simply didn't have the time to focus on this human aspect. It was up to me to find hard evidence. She had suffered multiple traumas as a kid, and the mitigation investigation turned up records. I found witnesses who could testify to a number of traumatic events in different chapters of her life. The attorneys continued to work with the other investigators, and ultimately, the prosecutor realized the police investigation wasn't strong. The mitigating evidence was icing on the cake. The attorneys were seasoned capital defense attorneys, and ultimately, got a deal Kelly could accept. Kelly never stopped questioning everything and advocating for her case. She didn't magically overcome the trauma she had suffered, but with the hard work we all put in, the members of her team were able to connect to each other. This trust was everything in Kelly's case.

For a mitigation specialist, the only difference between private and court appointed cases is who funds the mitigation investigation, the client or the court. Some teams will have unlimited resources available to them, others won't. In either scenario, resources to pay the criminal defense team may be limited. In an appointed case, the court will set a pre-authorized budget, paid for by taxpayers, and the finances of the court may vary as much as in private cases. Budget pressures, and willingness to allocate funds for defense teams, are different from district to district. In some jurisdictions, judges are still learning about mitigation, and the defense team will have to justify the cost to them. In many appointed cases, the resources allotted to the defense team are not adequate. Attorneys, this is where providing this book to judges may help your case.

In appointed cases, I strongly advise that every attorney automatically and immediately request funding for a mitigation specialist at the onset of a case. It can't be approved if it is never requested. Even when a mitigation specialist is appointed to the case, it's important to request realistic funding at the beginning. If, later in the case, the mitigation specialist needs more hours, the attorney must return to the judge to request more funds. Even if funds get denied, the attorney has done well to bring mitigation to the attention of the court. Writing a motion that gets denied still shows it's the system, not the attorney, standing in the way of proper representation for the accused. Denial may also prove to be a basis for an appeal later if needed.

So how many hours should the attorney request for mitigation investigation? In most felony cases, it's my opinion that 100 hours can get anything done. However, I've had felony cases assigned a budget of only 25-30 hours! In my experience, a typical budget for a felony case is about $600 to $2000 for the investigation. I know from my work that a mitigation investigation involves many hours of fieldwork — interviews, records retrieval, painstaking research, and follow up. In a private case with limited resources, or especially in an appointed case where the court hasn't allocated enough funding, the mitigation specialist will have to do what they can with what they have. Mitigation in all felony cases is the current trajectory of the field.

Since 2011, a majority of my cases have been court appointed. When more people understand mitigation, more private cases will include mitigation specialists. Most mitigation specialists I know consider the industry standard on death penalty cases to be 850 hours. On most capital murder cases, I work 400 hours within the first 6-8 months. In capital cases that go to trial, the number of hours can go up to 1,000 hours.

The death penalty has not always been the law of the land in the United States. There was a period between the 1960s and 1970s when no executions were carried out. As of 2025, 27 U.S. states retain the death penalty as a sentencing option. Many of those states have not executed a prisoner in recent times, but other states continue to carry out executions. As long as the death penalty is part of the system, mitigation in these cases is essential.

"Death is different"— that is how the saying goes in capital work. The judges are very aware of the difference. The prosecutors are going after both a guilty verdict and a death sentence. The defense must be fully prepared for a punishment phase hearing where a death sentence is a possibility. During the jury selection for a death penalty case, potential jurors must state on the record that giving a death sentence is possible for them. Since there is no going back after an execution, it's all hands-on deck on both sides in a death penalty case before sentencing. Mitigation in these cases is intense and expensive. It's not that other cases aren't as important or don't require diligence. It's just that these cases carry a special burden.

The American Bar Association (ABA) guidelines make mitigation mandatory in death penalty cases. In Texas, capital defense attorneys must reach a certain level of professional standard to be appointed to a death case. Attorneys who are qualified to represent capital defendants have many years of trial experience and apply to be on a list to be appointed to a capital case. Each county or state has their own vetting process to qualify an attorney to work these types of cases.

In a capital murder case, a *team* is appointed from the start: two attorneys, a mitigation specialist, and an investigator. The court will also allocate funding for expert testimony to educate the court about a variety of subject matters. These experts aren't advocates, they're teachers. They teach the court about their expertise.

The mitigation specialist and investigator work the case simultaneously. Mitigation must be much more in-depth in capital cases. These cases are long-term commitments as it could take up to five years to go to trial or get a plea offer.

Defending the person: Kevin
(all names are fictitious & details of the story altered for privacy)

Kevin took responsibility early on in his case. He was charged with capital murder. I have never met a man so remorseful. He was a mechanic, a father, a brother, a son, and a helper. If he could help you, he would. If he could make you smile, he would. In interviews, it was clear there were some painful events in his life that he didn't want to talk about. The events were so traumatic, he couldn't talk about them or even put his family through any more trauma by going to trial where they might be revealed. Kevin was remorseful and ready to plea, but the prosecutor didn't offer a plea for almost two years. At the beginning of the case, no one understood Kevin, what he lived through as a child, or how his brain had been damaged by trauma.

Kevin took responsibility early on in his case. He was charged with capital murder. I have never met a man so remorseful. He was a mechanic, a father, a brother, a son, and a helper. If he could help you, he would. If he could make you smile, he would. In interviews, it was clear there were some painful events in his life that he didn't want to talk about. The events were so traumatic, he couldn't talk about them or even put his family through any more trauma by going to trial where they might be revealed. Kevin was remorseful and ready to plea, but the prosecutor didn't offer a plea for almost two years. At the beginning of the case, no one understood Kevin, what he lived through as a child, or how his brain had been damaged by trauma.

Gradually, after building trust, I found out that Kevin's uncle had molested him and his brothers. Incest is not talked about. I discovered many men in his family had been molested by their elders. Words can't describe the pain I felt learning and holding this secret. We couldn't go to trial with this because the pain was too much for everyone. I felt like there had to be something else. I felt torn. The prosecutor continued to press for the death penalty without offering a plea. I wanted to protect Kevin and his family's privacy. If they wanted the incest to remain private I had honor it. I needed to keep looking for other mitigating factors.

Over the next weeks and months, I found records of head injuries. Interviews and records turned up evidence that pointed to brain trauma. The expert's evaluation lead the attorneys to ask the judge to approve money for a brain scan. Brain scans are expensive, and these requests are often turned down, but since Kevin was facing the death penalty, the judge approved it.

The brain scan showed evidence of multiple brain injuries. The defense attorneys saw first-hand how important a deep mitigation investigation is. It took a lot of trust to get to the truth, and we came close to not having anything to work with. The attorneys presented the brains scans to the prosecutor and the prosecutor knew this was convincing evidence. The prosecutor saw the brains scans a possible way for the jury to give a life sentence. The case was resolved in the way Kevin wanted, though a plea. He didn't have to go to trial and talk about the incest. His family was spared the ordeal of talking about it. The key in Kevin's case was the time factor needed to build relationships and find evidence.

Even though each case is different, there may be some common threads. The case will tell me. The people in the case will tell me. As a specialist with a lot of cases under my belt, I've learned what to look for. I know where to start. I do not know in what direction the story will lead me. That depends on the individuals. I listen with my heart. I follow my heart. The mitigation process will differ in each case: private, court-appointed, felony, or death penalty. Whether it goes to trial, or results in a plea before trial, understanding the mitigation investigation process will help the defense team, and the community around the case, and eventually the decision makers bring each case to a peaceful conclusion.

Chapter 5: The Mitigation Process

The mitigation investigation will be unique in every case, but each one will follow a process to answer the most difficult question about any crime: Why? The "why" investigation can take months to discover, so getting a mitigation specialist involved in the case as soon as the attorney is hired/appointed is crucial. The process will include different stages. Sometimes, the first phase of mitigation investigation takes place over a long period of time, before the other phases even begin. In other cases, the stages may overlap as the investigation continues. In general, the phases can be broken down into these steps: information gathering, pre-trial preparation, and/or trial. At any stage of the case, the attorney may ask for documents and reports as part of a mitigation presentation. Sometimes, that's the end of the mitigation specialist's work, but more often, the mitigation specialist is involved until the case is resolved.

Information Gathering

The mitigation investigation begins with a long phase of information gathering. There are different approaches, yet each case starts similarly: the attorney finds the mitigation specialist, introduces the team to the client or family, and the mitigation specialist requests records and builds rapport with clients and witnesses.

The mitigation specialist will meet with the client one-on-one multiple times. When first hired, most mitigation specialists know little about the client. The first visit is to listen to the client and get a release signed to start requesting records. Mitigation interviews may take two to three hours. Every interview will reveal a little bit more. Most people, not only the client, need multiple interviews to disclose information. The mitigation investigation is like a game of connect the dots, but the dots don't appear all at once. The picture the dots form will emerge later.

The client will share names of people who know them best. Those people will know other people who also might be able to help. The mitigation specialist will request records from schools, hospitals, other prisons, and the jail as well as disciplinary, medical, military, and civil court records, anything that helps put the puzzle together. The records will reveal other people who can provide information about the client's life. This might be a nurse, social worker, schoolteacher, probation officer, or someone close to the client, like a brother or best friend. The mitigation specialist gathers their stories through a series of interviews. Through investigation, interviews, record searches, and other sources, the mitigation specialist will piece together the client's life story.

I don't know how many times I've been asked - countless times - what I think the outcome of a case is going to be. I understand people are anxious and want certainty. Their life, or the life of someone they care about, is on the line. I don't know how any case will turn out. Sometimes people don't want to help someone they think might be guilty, so they ask me if he/she did it. Unless I have permission from the client, that's attorney-client privileged information, and I'm not free to divulge it. I'm not there to judge, guilty or not guilty. I'm working the case to ensure the attorney can tell my client's story and has access to all the information they need to defend their client properly. So, throughout this process, I ask all those involved to remember that everything centers around the client and their case.

It may seem like no progress is being made in this phase, but something absolutely crucial is being built: trust. The mitigation specialist will learn things about the client and will listen for people to interview, life circumstances, and places to request records. To the person on the outside, these interviews may seem more like conversations than formal interviews. No one discloses information until they feel safe. A mitigation specialist meets the person where they are. Every witness is an individual. Each witness has their own life. The mitigation specialist may meet with a witness more than once. This is normal. Mitigation is about building trust. I find that sometimes just sitting with a witness and being present is the best way to gain information. Listening is the best form of interviewing — it's actual medicine and therapeutic. Sometimes, significant events happened years ago, such as the onset of mental illness or trauma, and the person has blocked it out. This information will come out with time, patience and trust, of course.

Not everyone can spend time sitting down for an interview. A conversation may take place in a break room at work, or at people's homes while they do laundry, or in a car while they drive to their shift. Meeting a person where they are also means where they are emotionally. Sometimes people don't remember details at first. When people of the same family or community tell their story, commonalities begin to appear. The mitigation specialist will look for common threads that run through the interviews and records. They are always there. Not everybody says exactly the same thing, but more often than not, there is a strong mitigation theme, such as signs and symptoms of mental illness. If one person witnesses something, chances are there is someone else who reports similar symptoms. They may not tell the story in the same way, but the truth will be there.

Defending the person: Alvin
(all names are fictitious & details of the story altered for privacy)

Alvin's case was a difficult one. He seemed to be just your average guy, but his life had been riddled with "bad" behavior. Since age 14, he had been arrested multiple times. Some might say he was just a bad kid and then a bad man. But there was a lot more to Alvin's story. It takes compassion, and hard work, to seek out the truth of a person like Alvin. The prosecutor sought the death penalty for Alvin knowing that his IQ was 80 — above the score needed for waiver of execution for intellectual disability.

At first, it was not obvious that Alvin had brain injuries or even borderline intellectual problems. Alvin was the master of his life, a survivor. Compared to his siblings, he was thriving. He was used to hiding his disability by being fun-loving and connecting with people on an emotional level, especially women. He had developed skills to survive his deficits. His problems would sometimes overwhelm him and cause a lot of damage, to himself and others. When I started to dive deeper into the records, I found evidence of multiple mitigating factors. Alvin told me about a head injury when he was 14 years old. His head was slammed up against a wall in a juvenile detention center. I had to request records multiple times to find documentation of the bloody incident, but I finally did. All the juvenile records, taken as a whole, as difficult as they were to get from so many years back, began to come alive. I found more records of behaviors that pointed to a brain injury. We were getting close to trial, and we needed proof. The best way to get it was a brain scan. Based on the records we'd gathered, the attorney requested the brain scan and it was granted.

The scan found 17 brain injuries. Alvin's brain was so damaged that the report said he would suffer from injury-related dementia in less than ten years. The brain scans convinced the prosecutor to offer a plea before the case went to trial. I think the prosecutors understood that even if a jury gave him the death penalty, Alvin wouldn't be healthy enough to execute at the end of the day, so he offered a plea Alvin   could accept. The mitigation investigation looked below the surface and revealed the truth.

At some point, all the dots are on the page and the lines between the dots will begin to appear. A picture will emerge. The mitigation specialist has accumulated files of records, notes from witness interviews, and information from the client.   It now has to be organized. The mitigation specialist will use their professional insight and experience to organize the information into universal themes, ways the mitigation story can be told.

Plea Deals

I know talking about plea deals or punishment is upsetting, especially early in the case. It's still important to discuss how mitigation can make a difference in both plea deals and punishment, just in case. A football team gets ready for a whole game. They don't get to halftime and ask for time off to practice for the rest of the game. Their kickers practice for field goals even if they don't need them to win the game. A defense attorney can use mitigation investigation to prepare for plea negotiations with the prosecution. The attorney will advise the accused on the biggest decision of the case: whether to plead guilty or not guilty. The client knows enough about the indictment to decide. After an investigator does their job, the attorney knows how strong the defense is. Before a plea is entered, the attorneys may negotiate for a reduced sentence in exchange for a guilty plea. Most often, it's the prosecution who offers a plea bargain before the defense seeks one out.

Defense attorneys can reject the first offer and provide evidence, including mitigation, to back up their claims that a lesser sentence is justified. The mitigation investigation may uncover facts and information that influence the plea bargain. In some cases, but not all, the plea-bargaining phase includes some back and forth negotiations about a plea.

The defense can share what they might present at trial to discourage the prosecutor from going to trial. Keep in mind the prosecutor has their duty to fulfill, and they want to do a good job. It's important in plea negotiations for the prosecutor to feel like they are doing a good job. There is nothing wrong with the prosecutor feeling like a (s)hero. If they give a fair and just plea offer, they are (s)heroes. Not all prosecutors are bad people or the enemy. They too are humans, and mitigation gives them the opportunity to tap into their own humanity. The prosecutors are the gatekeepers in restorative justice.

A plea deal is reached when the defense accepts the prosecutor's offer of a specific punishment option (for example, probation or a certain number of years in prison) and enters that plea in court. If no plea bargain is offered, or the defense doesn't accept any offer, the case will go to trial, and a trial date will be set.

Defending the person: Sonny
(all names are fictitious & details of the story altered for privacy)

Sonny was 20 years old when he was arrested for aggravated robbery. In Texas, the range for punishment for robbery is from five to 99 years. This wide range gives the prosecutor a lot of options for charges and sentencing recommendations. In Sonny's case, the prosecutor was going for a maximum charge and punishment. The plea negotiations were stalled. I was brought into the case, and as I interviewed Sonny and his family, I could see he was redeemable. He had been, frankly, young and dumb, and the defense thought he should have a second chance, but, we needed to convince the prosecutor, who, after all, didn't know Sonny or his life circumstances like we did.

The mitigation investigation revealed that Sonny had lost a parent when he was eight. The surviving parent micromanaged the child, and Sonny grew up with a lot of self-doubt. He was trying to pull his life together, had a family, and was even in college. Every year, around the anniversary of his parent's death, his early childhood issues of trust and confusion would rear up. It was no coincidence that the crime happened right at that time. We put together a mitigation package explaining his family history and highlighting all the good things that were going on in Sonny's life. No excuses, just a way to show that there was hope for him. The prosecutor actually downgraded the charge and offered a plea.

Trial

The process of mitigation is the same whether a case results in a plea bargain or goes to trial. Both sides will put forward convincing information they have on their side. Mitigation benefits the trial process because it benefits the attorney's understanding of the human being they represent — not just the crime. At trial, mitigation gives the attorney tools to connect jurors to the client's life. In trial, there are two main phases: (1) the guilt/innocence phase and, if the verdict is guilty, (2) the punishment phase. The defense team should prepare for the punishment phase in every trial, but that doesn't mean they are expecting, or inviting, a guilty verdict. They are simply preparing a successful defense. As football or basketball teaches us, defense wins games. Effective representation of the client includes preparing for the punishment phase, no matter what. How the attorney uses the mitigating evidence and witnesses at the guilt or innocence stage of the trial, or any stage for that matter, is up to the attorney. Trust their best judgment. They will know how to build the case in all its parts.

Storytelling and narrative can connect strangers. Think of going to the movies, as the story unfolds, you find yourself drawn to a character. You may not have been expecting it, but you identify with the person, or the people, and you feel an emotional connection to the story. The character's story has come alive in you. Trial is where mitigation comes alive. Instead of unfolding on the screen and through action, the witnesses and the attorneys tell the story with their words. The attorneys and witnesses on the stand are having a dialogue. In some ways, the judge and jury are eavesdroppers. Just like you bring your own experiences and preferences into the movie theatre, the judge and jury bring theirs into a courtroom.

In the guilt-innocent phase, the prosecution builds their story. The burden to prove that story beyond a reasonable doubt is on the prosecutor. The defendant does not have to prove anything. Either the prosecutor proved the case beyond a reasonable doubt or they did not. The defendant doesn't even need to testify or present any evidence at all. The defendant may testify if they wish, but the burden always stays with the prosecutor to prove the case beyond a reasonable doubt. The judge explains this to the jury directly and clearly.

Mitigation is not like a trial in this respect. The bulk of mitigation evidence applies to punishment decisions. When the defense team engages in mitigation, they are telling the client's life story, either for the purpose of negotiating a disposition or plea, or for a sentencing presentation to get the lowest possible sentence. That requires presenting the powerful truth of the defendant's story along with the documentation and witnesses that support the mitigating factors.

The attorney will decide what information, and what story, to present to the decision makers. If a client is convicted, the punishment phase begins. In this phase also, defense attorneys can call witnesses to the stand and ask them questions to bring out the information of each witness. This is where the witnesses will get the chance to tell their truth about the client and the client's life. The prosecutor will also ask each witness questions.

During the punishment phase, the defense may also present "exhibits" — charts, a family tree, pictures, sentimental items. In order for these to be shown, a mitigation witness must introduce them and talk about them laying a foundation for their introduction. Once this evidence is shown the jury has it to look at later during deliberations.

Besides the mitigation witnesses who know the accused, the attorney can also call expert witnesses to educate the court. The experts testify because the attorney feels the jury needs to hear what research says about the mitigating circumstances. This expert testimony supports what other mitigating witnesses have said they saw in the life experiences of the accused. How does having an addicted father, or being molested by a neighbor, change a little kid's brain? How does the developing brain respond to these things? Only an expert who is qualified to testify can give this type of information to the jury or the judge.

An expert on childhood psychology can make a difference in the mind of certain jurors. I watched a trial one time where the expert used her research to give credibility to the defense's case. The client had been sent to an adult prison as a teenager. There were records proving that he had been sent to a certain facility at age sixteen. The expert had published research on how this exact kind of situation affects young people. A guard from the same prison, at the same time as the teenager was there, testified about the conditions. Each of these witnesses was an expert in their own way—one with publications and degrees to back up her credentials and the other with experiences and memories that painted a picture for the jury. By the end of the testimony, I could see that these witnesses had created understanding in the jurors' minds that they wouldn't have in any other way.

Professional or academic experts have to be paid for their time and expenses, which means the attorney in an appointed case has to request funding from the court. The mitigation specialist can give the attorney information and documents to make the case that the experts are needed. Experts are there to explain the science behind the "why" of the mitigation investigation. They are there to help create understanding. The funding for experts is well spent when it comes to making sure the whole truth is heard.

In recent years, mitigation has contributed to more life without parole sentences in capital murder cases.[10] Life without parole and death are the only options for jurors in capital cases. Mitigation in death penalty cases can be anything that inspires a juror to choose life over death for the client. Some examples could be what the client's family shared on the stand, the expert's testimony, in-jail conduct, a variety of mitigation themes, and remorse.

All the rapport and trust built throughout the case will pay off at trial. Witnesses for both the prosecution and the defense will show up because of their attachment to justice. The mitigation specialist discovers the mitigating factors by connecting the dots. The defense knows the truth, but that doesn't matter. What matters is that this truth gets told to the decision makers.

---

10 Gohara, Miriam, Grace Notes: A Case for Making Mitigation the Heart of Noncapital Sentencing , 41 Am. J. Crim. L. 41 (2013)

CHAPTER 6: MITIGATING EVIDENCE

The previous chapters have presented a general view of a mitigation investigation and how it brings about fair sentencing. I've shared stories, with names and details changed to protect privacy, of course, to explain how mitigation is not a concept, it is a practice. It affects real people from several different angles. It's a way of exploring the lives of people accused of a crime so that their defense includes who they are. Decision makers must know this to deliver true justice.

This chapter will get down to the details of mitigating factors. Each one of you may be involved in a case in a different way. Understanding the specifics of mitigating factors, and what the specialists are looking for when they interview the client, family members, and witnesses, will help the defense team. For attorneys and professional members of the team, knowledge of these precise issues will help you with various relationships. As a mitigation specialist, I often serve as the link between the legal professionals and the qualified experts on mental health. As the member of the team who investigates the client's life, I'm the one focused on uncovering mitigating evidence, and that evidence is most often about brain health.

Brain health, "a person's ability to function well in daily life and work,"[11] is the first and most important mitigating factor. Healthy brains do not hurt people. Good mitigation investigation will uncover all the elements in a person's life that have influenced their

---

[11] "What is Brain Health," The Center for Brain Health, University of Texas at Dallas, retrieved from https://brainhealth.utdallas.edu/what-is-brain-health/

decision-making. Mitigation themes related to brain health are centered around a person's ability to manage emotional stress. Healthy people have energy and skills to cope with life and relationships. People with unhealthy brains can let destructive thoughts take over their actions. That's the most simplistic way to explain how many criminal acts occur. The mitigation specialist is looking for evidence of brain health ailments in the records, evaluations, and the interviews. This evidence will be included in the mitigation package for the attorney. The mitigation specialist will present the best evidence available.

The tragedy is that in many, many cases in our courts, brain disorders are often present. Brain health is a major part of mitigation evidence because it affects culpability, or the blame a person deserves for not controlling their actions. Our system of justice takes mental health into account in deciding punishment. A person doesn't need to have extreme mental incapacity for the information on brain health to be a mitigating factor. Specifically, the mitigation specialist will be looking for descriptions and reports related to:

- mental illness
- behavior disorders
- trauma
- traumatic brain injury
- intellectual disability

Mitigation specialists are recognize context clues to the client's brain health in witness statements and records. Sometimes, the mitigation investigation uncovers a turning point in the life of the client. It can be an onset of mental illness, or a traumatic event, or a head injury, for instance.

Mental Illness and Behavioral Disorders

People don't report what is happening to them or their loved ones using the *Diagnostic and Statistical Manual of Mental Disorders* by the American Psychiatric Association. They use words they know to describe the person's behavior. The mitigation specialist will likely hear about paranoia, fear, anxiety, emotional outbursts, extreme highs and lows, confusion, dramatic changes in eating or sleeping habits, social withdrawal, and more, in everyday terms. People might use words like lazy, crazy, moody, drunk, bipolar, wild, lit, rude, etc. When the mitigation specialist hears these words, it's important to clarify what the person means.

The mitigation specialist is not a psychiatrist or a doctor, but they can recognize signs that a type of behavior should be investigated more. Evidence of these disorders can be reports from schools, doctors' records, eyewitnesses to behavior, prison records, anything. Sometimes, the mitigation investigation will turn up a diagnosis, but often, the person has gone without a diagnosis, or has been misdiagnosed. Sometimes a new expert evaluation is obtained. That diagnosis might be one piece of the puzzle, but as the mitigation specialist gathers information, she discovers there is more to the story than any one record shows.

Trauma

Trauma changes our brains. We remember trauma less in words and more with our feelings and our bodies. The mitigation investigation may turn up evidence of repeated trauma or a single traumatic event. The mitigation specialist must look at the whole life of the client. Traumatic events in childhood can have an impact on behaviors much later. The trauma can be ongoing, or can be one, or a few, events. Serious car accidents, natural disasters, injury, and abuse are all examples of trauma that can affect the brain.

Recent research has shown that there are actual physical changes in the brain after trauma. Specifically, these changes affect the brain's ability to react to later stress.[12] Brain scan research shows when we remember a traumatic event, the frontal lobe will shut down, and we get overwhelmed. The frontal lobe is the part of the brain that calms us down. It's the part that rationalizes that the loud bang sound came from a firecracker not a gun. If the frontal lobe is impaired permanently or temporarily, then the ability to self-calm is lost. This causes stimulus to trigger reactions that healthy brains can filter out.

The mitigation investigation will look for evidence that trauma has occurred that has changed the brain in this way. It is not looking for an excuse for the crime. It's putting together a picture of a whole person who was damaged by trauma in a way that impacts their decision making and their actions. Many studies have documented that exposure to trauma increases the chance of arrest and incarceration.[13] Documents, records, and witness accounts that detail traumatic events are important evidence.

Brain Injury

The mitigation specialist may discover evidence of a physical injury to the brain. To introduce this as mitigating evidence, the defense attorney may need to hire a neuropsychologist to perform an evaluation. This evaluation will confirm that the brain has a current effect from the injury such as a deficit in the speed and (in)accuracy of brain processing or memory. The evaluation could lead to a possible request for a brain scan. In cases of traumatic events, a brain injury can change or influence a person's behavior. If documentation of when and how the brain injuries occurred exists, it's

12 Bremner J. D. (2006). Traumatic stress: effects on the brain. *Dialogues in Clinical Neuroscience*, 8(4), 445–461.
13 Jäggi LJ, Mezuk B, Watkins DC, Jackson JS. The Relationship between Trauma, Arrest, and Incarceration History among Black Americans: Findings from the National Survey of American Life. *Soc Ment Health*. 2016; 6(3):187–206. doi:10.1177/2156869316641730

the mitigation specialist's job to locate it. It may take time and painstaking research to find the hard evidence, but it can be done with adequate funding and, of course, trust.

Intellectual Disability

Another factor that a mitigation investigation can uncover is intellectual disability. In many cases, the person has never had a formal diagnosis, but evidence begins to emerge that suggests that the person has this type of deficit. Witnesses will tell stories of laziness, a lack of personal hygiene, emotional disturbances at school or work, mooching off people, not paying bills, etc. These can all point to a deficiency in life skills called adaptive behaviors. Adaptive behaviors are the skills we use to function in our everyday lives. People can become very good at covering up a deficit in adaptive behaviors, just as people who can't read overcome and adapt. The clues to a lack of adaptive behaviors may be subtle. Intellectual disability is about what the person can't do, not what they can do. The mitigation specialist is looking for information about trouble with everyday tasks the person might have had as far back as elementary school. That is when teachers and caregivers can be helpful mitigation witnesses. When this evidence begins to come to light, the investigator will refer the accused for an evaluation. Intellectual disability is proven through an expert's evaluation. The law wants an IQ score and what is called an "adaptive behaviors assessment."

Even if the client is older, proving intellectual disability in a criminal case must contain evidence from before age 18. For example, finding a childhood label of emotional disturbance (school records) can prove that the client had an adaptive behavior deficit before age 18. They must also have a lower IQ number and proof of adaptive behavior deficit(s).

Experts

Sometimes the mitigation investigation turns up information that merits further examination by professionals in specific areas. The mitigation specialist is on the front lines of accumulating this information. When enough evidence has been gathered, the attorney will want to hire an expert on the specific subject matter. This expert can diagnose, describe, and testify about the factors in depth.

At the end of the day, investigating the mystery behind the actions of the client takes into consideration the developmental process of the mental condition for this individual person. The mitigation specialist, or the attorney, will decipher the information and how to use it to get the best results for the client. Mental health ailments, brain injuries, and trauma have a profound effect on the way a person functions in life. A person with a brain ailment processes right and wrong differently from a person with a healthy brain. Considering brain health, or the lack thereof, is not new in the American justice system. All of these are some of the mitigating factors that could be presented to the court by the attorney when they tell the client's story.

Decision makers can relate to the client's humanity if the evidence is presented to them in a way that makes sense. The witnesses, the client, the records, the experts are all the dots that the mitigation specialist will connect to create a picture of the accused's actions, brain health and life circumstances. The mitigation specialist shares the evidence of mitigating factors by providing the defense attorneys with a mitigation package. Just like every case is different, every mitigation package will vary. The next chapter will describe some of the documents that can go into a mitigation package. The exact form of the reports, how many copies, which original reports get included, all the details of exactly what goes into the package is up to the lead attorney.

CHAPTER 7: THE MITIGATION PACKAGE

Once the mitigation investigation comes to a close, a story has emerged. The dots are connected, and the mitigation specialist will prepare a mitigation package for the attorneys. The lead attorney will decide, with help from the team members, what needs to be included. Some attorneys want all the records at their fingertips, others only want the important pages. The mitigation specialist will often write up a mitigation report that sums up the most important themes and supporting evidence. Sometimes, there is a "narrative," or a chart, or a punishment phase run-down. Because each case follows its own path, what goes into the package may change as the case develops. At this stage, the attorney and the witnesses will have built enough trust with the mitigation specialist to put together the best package possible.

The attorney will want to present a coherent storyline to the decision makers that humanizes the client and creates understanding around the alleged crime. The mitigation specialist will deliver to the attorney various mitigation tools for this purpose. These are documents and reports that help the attorney tell the story. They will differ in every case.

Witnesses and Records

A witness list is a list of the mitigation witnesses, including contact information, their relationship with the client, and a description of the information they have or can provide. A record log sets out all the records in the case and whether they have been received or still need to be requested. It also includes the source of the records and contact information.

Chronology

The chronology is a list of major events or milestones in the client's life in time order. It shows a connect flow of life events. This document will have a column for each entry: date, data, and source of information. It can include information such as life events, the client's birthday, family members' birthdays, graduation, a marriage, a death in the family, the date of a head injury, a car accident, a traumatic event, anything that might affect the client emotionally or physically. It is a quick reference tool for the attorney to see where to find the information they may want to bring out in trial.

Trial Rundown

The trial rundown is the road map of the trial before it starts, a chronological order of witnesses and exhibits for the punishment phase. Think of it like the storyboard for a movie; it gives the attorney a way to build the case for mitigation through a storyline. There will be a column for each subject: witness and contact information, answers to the questions that will be asked, and the dates of interviews of the witnesses.

Family Tree

A family tree may not be used in every case, but it can show decisions makers, like jurors, who the client is related to. It acts as another tool for humanizing the accused. At its best, it shows the jury the faces of the client's loved ones. It can show pictures, such as school photos or family group photos, or it might even have pictures of the homes the client grew up in. The family tree can be color coded to make it easier for the jury to understand.

Narrative

The narrative of the client's life is an account of connected events written out as a story. The best narratives help the attorney paint a picture of the client's life to the decision makers. The attorney chooses how to use this information. The narrative should contain just the facts and not conclusions or grand ideas about the state of our society. The true story of the client is what you want the decision makers to understand. The narrative can lead them to empathy. Storytelling at its best is based on the truth.

Affidavits

The affidavits are written, sworn statements by a variety of witnesses. They give the attorney an idea of what these witnesses would say if they were to testify in court. Sometimes these affidavits are used in the plea-bargaining stage and can be put together in a package to present to the judge and/or prosecutor. The affidavits should be under two pages long because, let's face it, judges and prosecutors are busy people, and they aren't likely to read long, rambling statements.

Character Letters

Witnesses may get a character letter guide and mitigation specialists may initiate a character letter campaign. These letters are specific to requesting grace and mercy from the prosecutor or judge. The attorney will decide who is the target audience.

Records

The mitigation specialist will also provide hard copies of records, usually just one or two pages each, that the attorney can use as evidence to support a mitigating theme. For instance, if the attorney presents expert witnesses on intellectual disability, the mitigation specialist will provide the test results in hard copy form or a school record that supports the test results from before the client was 18 years old. There could be business records, school reports, or medical records, for instance. These are the "proof" supporting the mitigating themes. This hard evidence needs to be organized so that the attorney can find it easily.

Mitigation Report

Each attorney likes to receive information differently. A good mitigation report begins with the history of client's life in paragraph form. Then the mitigation specialist's professional opinion or the results of the mitigation investigation is written next. The best mitigation reports highlight the strongest mitigating evidence such as childhood development, neuroscience, parenting issues, poverty, and mitigating circumstances around the crime. They should include references to where the documentation for these topics can be found, in which records or interview memos, pictures or research. Then they conclude with the sentencing recommendations and the strongest arguments for the attorney to consider presenting to the decision makers.

The mitigation specialist is just that — a specialist. The mitigation specialists are the experts in what the evidence points to as mitigating factors. They understand and have developed the themes and the issues. Their job is to organize this information for the attorney and to give their insights on how witnesses or mitigation evidence could support the mitigating theme(s).

CHAPTER 8: WORKING IN OUR CRIMINAL JUSTICE SYSTEM

Mass incarceration affects everyone, just like crime affects everyone. To me, mass incarceration is itself a crime. It is a crime against humanity. The current conditions were created long before you were born, and fixing it will take time. There have been many books written on the problem of mass incarceration, and I recommend anyone interested in reform learn more about it.

I have first-hand knowledge of the effects of mass incarceration as a professional mitigation specialist and from the people I know in prison. Most of my clients are in prison for long-term stays and some for the rest of their lives. Thankfully, none are on death row. Seeing a person in cuffs and knowing they live in a cage wears on a person's psyche, even though I know I get to leave and go home to my family.

When I visit a jail, it's packed, it is uncomfortable, it stinks, and it's loud. No one can catch a break in there. No one is at ease. Every jail visit is a reminder of the disease of systematic racism. It is a reality check of just how incarceration dehumanizes our people. The facts are that our prisons are overflowing, we have one of the highest rates of incarceration in the industrialized world, and since the 1980s, prison sentences have sharply increased in length. And those burdens have fallen heaviest on people of color.[14] Our criminal justice system

---

14 For additional statistics on comparative incarceration rates for the U.S. with other countries, as well as breakdowns of sentencing lengths and racial inequities, see The Sentencing Project, Criminal Justice Facts, 2020, https://www.sentencingproject.org/criminal-justice-facts/.

targets and punishes black and brown people and people living in the crisis of poverty more harshly than the privileged.[15]

In the courtroom, I've seen with my own eyes how many people in orange jumpsuits don't have the resources or fame to get the attention or the second chance or the mental health care they deserve. Especially all the young people whose brains are not fully developed, which I know from my experiences is not often even considered as a factor in young people's cases. In 2017, a judge thanked the defense attorney because the information I included in the mitigation packet helped educate the court on the basics of frontal lobe development.

I meet, greet and interact with people who can't bring themselves to the realization that systematic racism exists. I say "can't" because it's my understanding that they don't have the life experiences or life inflictions to understand what is really happening to other people. Even though I think this type of person might lack the ability to put themselves in someone else's shoes, I treat them humanely. I have to reach deep down in myself to have empathy for their *need* for discovery, just like I would anyone else. Honestly, I don't feel an urge to scold, teach, educate, or argue with those who I see as being in denial. All I can do is challenge people to have compassion for my clients. That means while I work on behalf of my client, my professional conduct includes consideration of everyone I interact with. I know that I am either a part of the problem or a part of the solution.

I've actually been advised in my work against having hope or giving hope to clients and their families. I understand the need to be realistic. I still have hope myself, and I

---

15 For more information on the racial and economic disparities in sentencing, see the Sentencing Project Report to the United Nations on Racial Disparities in the US Criminal Justice System, 2018, https://www.sentencingproject.org/publications/un-report-on-racial-disparities/. Racial disparities in the federal system have also been documented, for example, in DB Mustard's Racial, Ethnic, and Gender Disparities in Sentencing: Evidence from the U.S. Federal Courts*, https://www.journals. uchicago.edu/doi/abs/10.1086/320276. For a discussion on the effects of income inequality, see https://nij.ojp.gov/library/publications/economic-inequality-and-discrimination-sentencing.

share that hope out of my desire to meet people where they are in life. I let go of the expectation   others can meet me where I am. I believe in people and this human experience so strongly that just doing that one thing - meeting people where they are physically, mentally and spiritually - gives me the freedom to help my clients. My hope comes from knowing that I am doing my best and believing anyone I meet is doing their best no matter the reality. My hope is an exercise of faith. In an acknowledgment to have and give hope, I have to be open to learning from the people I meet.

I dislike long, harsh punishments because I understand they could be avoided if holistic rehabilitation were part of our system. My work has reduced sentences and prevented death as a form of punishment. Mitigation used on a mass scale has the power to reduce sentencing overall.

In 2003, the step of making mitigation mandatory in death penalty cases was just the beginning. It was a necessary step for the bar association, not an end goal. In addition to my own practice, I've used my resources to get the word out in every way I can. There are other private practitioners, like myself, working to further the use of mitigation in their communities, and it has been my honor to meet them. When I saw that there was a lack of mitigation specialists, I put at least $20,000 into creating an online training course. I've appeared several times on the local Pacifica radio station's "Prison Show" and answered questions from incarcerated people. I've consulted other mitigation specialists on their cases. I've given talks in national social worker seminars, law schools, prisons, and in college courses.

Now, I'm pouring my time and effort into this book for the families like those I represent and for their legal representatives. This book is not necessarily a call to action. My goal is to initiate a shift in the filter of your mind, a change in viewpoint. This book is an invitation to be part of the solution.

Sharing information and being accessible to my community is my part. It's going to take a variety of partnerships for mitigation investigation to be a part of all cases. It's going to take more education both by professionals and by the people most affected by our racist system. Professionals will need to realize the role they play in mass incarceration. People, professionals, advocates, and decision makers will have to create and support nonprofits to provide mitigation. It will take grant money allocated to mitigation initiatives, judge-granted court-appointed mitigation specialists, and attorneys applying mitigation in every case. Law schools must include mitigation training in their course offerings. Families, and the accused, will have to know about mitigation and want to take an active role. They will have to accept the invasive nature of mitigation, even embrace it. They must advocate for use of mitigation. All these things take time.

Mitigation evidence has the power to influence the decision maker for the proper sentence for the accused person. Once a sentence is handed down by the judge and the jury, it takes triple the work to get it changed. Mitigation is how working professionals are fighting for justice at the trial level. When a mitigation specialist looks for records, they are tipping the scales of justice toward a balance. When they interview witnesses, they are working for the greater good.

I have noticed that knowing that the system isn't fair makes victories that much sweeter. Whatever victory looks like depends on you. A life sentence may not seem like a victory to some, but if the only other choice is a death sentence, it is. Mitigation is the way I help bring about victories in criminal cases. I hope you see where you can apply, or encourage others to apply, mitigation to criminal cases. Mitigation is a solution waiting its turn in the criminal justice reform line, and while we wait, can you be a part of justice for someone? That's a very personal question. The answer is: it depends. It is up to each individual, each person and situation. We each define justice in our own way.

Anyone reading this book might be a potential juror one day, and I want you to be curious about mitigation. If it is missing, understand that the accused person is not getting a fair trial. This system will shift and change as the people operating in it change. We, the people, are the ones who commit the crimes and love the people charged with committing crimes. We are the ones who sit in a jury box determining a punishment. We, the people, have no choice but to operate within an unjust system. Mitigation done properly is one way to restore integrity in the system. Justice cannot happen without us—it is "just us!"

CONCLUSION

This book was created from my desire for all of us to know more about mitigation and make each other accountable as a people. Now you have a better understanding of what mitigation evidence is and how to get it. Records are important, but so are you, the community around the accused person. Experts are important, but mitigation witnesses are the real experts on the life of the client. You read about mental health and behavior health and how that applies to criminal defense. If the client feels ignored, they are not getting the attention they need and maybe have been put in a box and are not being looked at as a human being. The client should stand up for themselves or someone needs to stand up for them. You will also be fighting for those who will come behind you!   I hope this book has given you the information and the strength to do that. You now know more about each role of the criminal defense team, so you know what to ask of them and how to support them. You now know more about the resources available in each case. You now know more about the process mitigation uses to bring about a fair outcome. That does not mean you, no matter what your role, can sit back and take the process for granted. You are a part of it. This book is one of many ways to share mitigation with you – you are part of the change I want to see in the world. Here you've learned about mitigation evidence, practices, and procedures that have worked to bring my clients their individual punishments for their crimes and to avoid the death penalty.

I look forward to the days coming when a person is sentenced with the consideration of who they are as a person— as the law requires. This book is a tool to make informed choices in criminal defense, specifically the ones who get a personal opportunity to affect the coming changes. These shared experiences are my gift to you to fight for justice. When we believe in our common humanity,

fair sentencing and alternative routes to punishment will keep people out of prison. We are changing by becoming informed and making different choices with our money, with our vote, and with our energy. Each case I've worked on has proven to me that narrative, unity, and integrity is the winning formula for justice. By appreciating the humanity in another person, the decision makers can recognize their own humanity. This book may seem to only be about practical application for criminal defense but it's also about changing lives. If you can be a part of this change, please do.

APPENDIX

Table 1 is a fraction of Texas criminal cases, prioritized by which client got the least to the most mitigation investigation. When reviewing the chart, consider the charge and the punishment. Consider the date of the crime and how long before or after the crime that the ABA guidelines introduced mitigation to the field of criminal defense. Keep in mind that we do not know all there is to know about each person convicted. Court documents sometimes provide details of a given trial and mitigation investigation or lack thereof. There are many factors that go into a mitigation investigation, and each case is unique to the person accused, their defense team, the county in which the crime occurred, the District Attorney, and judge and/or jury. So many factors are major considerations in the outcome of each case. This table showcases where our defense community has evolved and is evolving to. Table 1 is not meant to be anything more than an educational tool for the reader to see how mitigation works and to provide the reader with insight on the practice.

The first ten cases, unfortunately, are cases in which mitigation was not available to the client or was limited in some way. MacDonald was charged with aggravated sexual assault, and the trial court refused to give the client a mitigation specialist. The trial attorney attempted to hire a person who was a counselor, yet counseling and mitigation are inherently different. MacDonald was sentenced to life and appealed it.

The attorney assigned to Lopez's case failed to investigate and present mitigation evidence, and in 2013, the appellate courts ruled in Lopez's favor to give him a resentencing. Winning that case opened the door for more mitigation in non-capital cases. Yet, ten years earlier, Alfaro's trial attorney did not investigate, nor present mitigation, and he received several sentences, totaling 150 years.

In the midsection of Table 1 are cases that had mitigation, but its use was limited or mismanaged. The Gonzales case included mitigation through a defense expert. This is a prime example of where the actual use of mitigation is so important. The testifying expert, Dr. Milam, diagnosed Mr. Gonzales, explaining that he had signs and symptoms of reactive attachment disorder because of the client's relationship with his mother when he was very young. This could lead a juror to think a person will never be able to change. Dr. Milam explained Gonzales' disorder was due entirely to environmental factors, whereas as a young child, Mr. Gonzales was not able to form a stable, emotional bond with any adult figure. Moreover, this led to immature, insecure, solitary, and manipulative tendencies, displayed by Mr. Gonzales later in life. The jury was to decide whether this part of Mr. Gonzales' past was mitigating or aggravating. The jury was responsible for deciding the punishment for Mr. Gonzales, and the jury granted him death.

The bottom ten cases benefited more from mitigation because the capital murder defendants did not receive the death penalty. Compare this with the capital cases at the top of the chart, which received a death sentence. Reyes, Gibbs, and Johnson did not receive any mitigation investigation until a considerable amount of time after the crime was committed. Reyes and Gibbs had the death penalty waived. The Johnson case went to trial, and the jury gave the accused life without parole. The Johnson case received hundreds of hours of mitigation investigation, which helped because the members of the trial team changed in 2017. Consider that the lower ten cases were more than ten years after the ABA guidelines were implemented, that mitigation is standard in all capital cases, and that more attorneys are learning how to use, and maximize, the outcomes of mitigation. Adams, Heath, and Tiharihondi were able to get the death penalty waived as a form of punishment early in the case due to effective mitigation.

Table 1 Ordered from top to bottom: least mitigation to most mitigation investigation:

Case Name	Year of Crime	Charge
MacDonald v. State	2014	Aggravated Sexual Assault
Lopez v. State	2013	Aggravated Robbery
Murphy v. Davis	2000	Capital Murder
Exparte Alfaro	2003 2007	Continuous Sexual Abuse of a Child
Green v. State	2013	Indecency with a Child
Chanthakoummane v. Stephens	2006	Capital Murder
Johnson v. State	2013	Capital Murder
Davis v. State	2012	Capital Murder
Gonzales v. Stephens	2001	Capital Murder
Cade v. State	2011	Capital Murder

(continued from left)

Mitigation Investigation	Sentence
In this case the court refused to appoint a "mitigation expert." The trial attorney hired a counselor who was not qualified to replace the role of a mitigation specialist.	Life
The attorney failed to investigate and present any mitigation evidence at sentencing, even when the sentencing was a plea deal.	30 Years
The client lost the appeal. However, the trail attorney was "procedurally barred" on claims for failing to hire mitigation expert	Death
Trial counsel failed to investigate and present mitigating evidence at the punishment phase of trial. This was one of many arguments on the list of ineffective assistance.	150 Years
The trial attorney did not call any mitigation witnesses.	20 Years
The trial attorneys had not thoroughly investigated the client's background to provide mitigating evidence. Also, the definition of mitigation at the time unconstitutionally impacted the outcome of his trial. The higher court did not agree. The death sentence remained intact.	Death
The defendant (appellate attorney) argued that the jury was improperly selected regarding how they would consider/weigh mitigating evidence.	Death
Mitigation investigation was performed and presented at trial. The defendant (appellate attorney) argued the definition of mitigation was not adequate and wanted the court to instruct the jury on how to weigh the mitigating evidence.	Death
Mitigation investigation was performed and presented at trial including expert testimony. The defense expert testified to both mitigating and aggravating details of the client's life.	Death
Mitigation investigation was performed and presented at trial. The higher court denied appeal as it found the standard for mitigation was fulfilled and jury instruction was complete.	Death

Table 1 continued from previous page

Case Name	Year of Crime	Charge
State v. Gibbs	2010	Capital Murder
State v. Reyes	2011	Capital Murder
State v. Johnson	2013	Capital Murder
State v. Burleson	2015	Capital Murder
State v. Adams	2012	Capital Murder
State v. Heath	2016	Capital Murder
State v. Tiharihondi	2015	Capital Murder
USA v. Fellows	2018	Sexual Assault of Child
State v. Nwanne	2017	Aggravated Robbery
State v. Ligas	2015	Capital Murder

(continued from left)

Mitigation Investigation	Sentence
Mitigation investigation was performed years after the crime.	30 Years
Mitigation investigation was performed years after the crime.	Life Without Parole
Mitigation investigation was performed years after the crime.	Life Without Parole By Jury
District Attorney waived the death penalty as a form of punishment after 1 year of mitigation investigation.	Life Without Parole
Mitigation investigation began around the time of the crime. Mitigation facts waived the death penalty. The Prosecutor then offered a plea.	Life Without Parole
Mitigation investigation began around the time of the crime. Mitigation facts waived the death penalty after one year of investigation.	Life Without Parole
Mitigation investigation began around the time of the crime. Mitigation facts waived the death penalty and Prosecutor offered a plea deal after one year of investigation.	Life Without Parole
Mitigation investigation began around the time of the crime. Mitigation facts waived a life sentence as the punishment. The Prosecutor agreed to cap (set a maximum on) the sentence.	27 Years
Mitigation facts down grade charge so the Prosecutor was then able to recommend probation.	Probation
Mitigation investigation began around the time of the crime. Mitigation facts waived the death penalty; Judge (as opposed to a jury) sentenced the client.	15 Years

Mitigation investigation is growing accepted practice. It is not until a defendant is convicted of a crime, and actually goes to prison, that they are able to appeal their case. Most appeals are funded by families of the defendant and not usually by a public or private non-profit or government agency. The more appeals won on the grounds of mitigation rulings the better. However, there are many grounds for winning an appeal. It depends on the case.

To win an ineffective assistance of counsel claim, the defendant must prove that they did not get the representation that the constitution demands at the trial level. Mitigation appeal claims are only as good as the case law that comes before it. Winning an appeal means a higher court reviewed the lower court's proceeding and sentence and decided that the case be re-tried or re-sentenced because of error(s) at the trial level. If an appeal is won, the case will go back to the lower court to be re-tried or resentenced.

Only when the appeal is won because a judge of the higher court made a ruling, can new case law be made and developed by trial attorneys at the trial level. Appeals are limited to certain cases because most defendants simply cannot afford an appellate attorney to review their case. Most people who are in prison post-conviction were living in the crisis of poverty at the time of their trial.

Table 2 Some case law supporting the hire of mitigation specialists and using their investigation findings

Opinion Date	Name of Case	Case Law Details
1984	Strickland v. Washington, 455 U.S. 688	This case determines if or when a criminal defendant's 6th amendment right to counsel is violated by their counsel's performance at any stage of the case.
1998	Moore v. State, 983 S.W.2d 15	In this case, appellant's trail counsel presented no evidence of mitigating factors for the jury to balance against the aggravating factors presented by the state. Indeed, appellant's trail counsel performed no investigation into any possible mitigating factors and failed to contact even a single family member or friend, despite the availability of such mitigation evidence.
2000	Milburn v. State, 15 S.W.3d 267, 270	Counsel is ineffective when he fails to see out, investigate, and interview available witnesses during the punishment phase.
2003	Wiggins v. Smith, 539 U.S. 510	Wiggins was represented by the Maryland public defender who discovered extremely helpful records. However, the public defender did nothing with those records. The Supreme Court ruled there is a duty to thoroughly investigate and follow through with the investigation of mitigating factors.
2005	Shanklin v. State, 190 S.W.3d 154	Failure to uncover and present mitigating evidence cannot be justified as a tactical decision when defense counsel has not conducted a thorough investigation of the defendant's background.
2005	Rompilla v. Beard, 545	Rompilla's trial counsel was ineffective for failing to make reasonable efforts to examine the file on Rompilla's prior convictions: rape and assault. Moreover, counsel had known the prosecution would probably present the prior conviction to the jury during sentencing. In that file counsel would have found mitigation evidence about Rompilla's troubled childhood and mental health.
2012	Lafler v. Cooper, 566 U.S. 166	Defendant has the right to an effective lawyer during plea stage of the case. The lawyer must disclose the prosecution's plea offer to the client.
2018	McCoy v. Louisiana, 138 S.Crt 1500	The lawyer must consider the client's concerns and ideas in presenting evidence or not. The client is a part of the decision-making process for the case.

Website: https://mitigationuniversity.com/

Mitigation University offers a series of videos on mitigation investigation for criminal cases. These practical techniques and know-how can be used in everyday practices to help build an effective case.

Mitigation University was created to showcase the investigation techniques of one mitigation specialist, in the hope to assist and support other practitioners, and to encourage mitigation investigation to be used in all criminal cases.

As mitigation can be used in a variety of settings, this course is suitable for any professional preparing for punishment trials, plea bargains or death-waivers in capital murder cases.